Count All the Way to Sesame Street

By Dina Anastasio · Illustrated by Richard Brown

Inspired by SESAME STREET PRESENTS: FOLLOW THAT BIRD,
screenplay by Tony Geiss and Judy Freudberg

This educational book was created in cooperation with the Children's Television Workshop, producers of Sesame Street. Children do not have to watch the television show to benefit from this book. Workshop revenues from this product will be used to help support CTW educational projects.

A SESAME STREET / GOLDEN PRESS BOOK

Published by Western Publishing Company, Inc. in conjunction with
Children's Television Workshop.

GREETINGS! I am the Count, and I am going to tell you a story about one big bird. Yes, that's right! **One** wonderful big bird who lives on Sesame Street. Big Bird is his name.

2

Every day Big Bird went to Hooper's Store and had **two** delicious birdseed sundaes.

And every day he played baseball with his friends.
Three friends playing baseball. Big Bird was happy on
Sesame Street.

But a busybody bird named Miss Finch decided that Big Bird would be happier living with other birds. She sent him off to live with a family of **four** Dodo birds.

Life with the Dodos was not like life on Sesame Street. Every time the **five** birds sat down to dinner, Big Bird missed his friends. The Dodos had terrible table manners. Big Bird decided to go back home to Sesame Street.

Six Kermits on the six o'clock news on six television sets said that Big Bird had run away! He was trying to find his way back to Sesame Street.

Seven of us set out from Sesame Street to find Big Bird.
I counted my friends. I counted myself. Yes, there were
seven searchers, looking for Big Bird.

I stopped to wait for a train to pass. I counted **eight** cars in the train. I had to count them very fast because the train was in a big hurry.

Then I passed a farm. I didn't see Big Bird, but I saw **nine** fantastic haystacks in the field.

I looked for Big Bird in the Fun Fair Carnival. I counted **ten** magnificent horses on a merry-go-round, but no Big Bird.

I stopped to wait for a parade to pass. Wonderful! I
love a parade. I counted **eleven** marchers in the Toadstool
Parade.

Wait! One of those marchers looked familiar.

Everyone on Sesame Street was delighted to see
Big Bird again. **Twelve** happy Sesame Street friends:
1, 2, 3, 4, 5, 6, 7, 8, 9, 10, 11, 12!
"Welcome home, Big Bird!" we all said.
Wonderful!